ICON: *St. Nicholas Novgorod.*   XV Century
Lent by Mr. George Riabov, New York

A Survey of
RUSSIAN PAINTING
Fifteenth Century to the Present

The Gallery of Modern Art
Including the Huntington Hartford Collection
New York
14 June — 17 September 1967

Cover: NATHALIE GONTCHAROVA. *Costume Design for "Le Coq d'Or": A Man.* 1914
Lent by Mr. George Riabov, New York
Copyright Foundation for Modern Art, 1967

FOREWORD

The Gallery of Modern Art is proud, indeed, to present the first comprehensive survey of Russian painting to be held in this country. Although we drew only upon American collections, in the awareness that our representation would be incomplete, we felt that the need was evident, and the moment opportune, to acquaint ourselves with the aspirations of the Russian people as revealed in their art. We hope that this exhibition will be the first word in a dialogue of artistic exchange, a dialogue which will require continuing effort but which is certain to reward both our nations with increased understanding of our different histories and our similar goals.

Museums are concerned with historical evidence and its profound revelations; people are interested in their own time. We have included in this survey a number of works by contemporary Russian artists in the belief that the works are worth seeing in America, not only for their intrinsic merit but also for their important communication of an intense commitment to the artists' homeland and native traditions. Some of the artists are more aware than others of recent trends in the West. Those who are may respond to a kindred spirit, but they follow no idols slavishly. There is no common attitude toward subject matter or style among these contemporary painters; their unity derives from a common loyalty to their own natures and experience, whether expressed in abstract or representational forms. In the historical context of this survey of Russian painting, their integrity and dedication to the essential goals of their profession becomes more evident.

It is with great pleasure that we express our gratitude for the generous cooperation of the lenders, many of Russian descent, to our exhibition. We owe the deepest gratitude to George Riabov of the Museum of Modern Art, who has organized this exhibition with a scholarly knowledge and a native passion for Russian art which have overcome the many obstacles to his task. It is with respect that one can record the opinion that Russians remain Russians, whatever their current geographical location.

MARGARET POTTER
Curator and Acting Director

ICON: *St. John the Evangelist.*   XVI Century
Lent by the Brooklyn Museum, New York

4

This exhibition celebrates Russian painting, including its creative peak of the fifteenth and sixteenth centuries, the process of transition and growth, the innovating phase of modern art and the present-day achievement. It seems fortunate that this exhibition, the first in the United States to present the whole range of the development of Russian painting, may help to focus attention upon the Russian contribution to the world of art. The Russians are not only medieval icon painters who could create brilliant images of the unchangeable Divine Order of extraordinary emotional and spiritual impact, but they are also masters of modern art who have presented in new visual images the contemporary life of constant change.

The exhibition has been designed to present as comprehensive as possible a showing of Russian painting as space and availability of material in this country would permit. The selection is not absolutely a qualitative one, as the exhibition does not draw from such vast depositories of Russian painting as the Tretyakoff Gallery of Moscow and the Russian Museum of Leningrad, but only from museums, private collections and galleries outside of Russia. It is with a deep-felt sense of its inadequacy that this exhibition is offered. While most of the major periods of Russian painting from the fifteenth through the twentieth centuries are represented, this exhibition makes no pretense to be a definitive survey of Russian art. The different periods and painters are represented by two or more examples of their work; however, some, unfortunately, are shown by less significant works, while some could not be included at all. For instance, works by the greatest icon painter, *Andrey Rublev* (ca. 1360-1430) and the lonely giant of modern Russian painting, *Mikhail A. Vrubel* (1856-1910) were not available in this country. It is hoped, however, that the esthetic expression of the available examples will give the American public a microscopic view of Russian painting and show its contribution to European culture of values which have a permanent significance for the development of art.

A thousand years of shifting ascendancy of influences of classical antiquity and Byzantium, of the East and the West, have altered the outward semblance, but not the inner spirit, of Russian art. Russian artists at all times have learned to discriminate among the cultures infiltrating from neighboring peoples and to assimilate that which appealed to them. Foreign concepts were reshaped into an integrated entity and given a definite Russian spirit. Foreign artists working in Russia were affected by the acute Russian sensibility and individuality, and they also transformed their idioms to accommodate the Russian spirit.

Emerging both from fun and color-loving toilers of the soil and from the austere hieratic ruling class dominated by the Greek Orthodox Church, Russian art remained ecclesiastical and medieval long after the art of the West had become secularized and concerned with the visual conquest of nature. Medieval artistic principles remained obvious in Russia up to the time of Peter the Great's reforms. However, whatever the speed of growth of Russian art into a fully self-conscious and highly developed state, thus far it has been more or less gen-

ICON: *Royal Sanctuary Doors (pair).* XVI Century
Lent by A La Vieille Russie, Inc., New York

EVGRAF P. CHEMESOV. *Catherine the Great Mourning the Death of Elisabeth.* Ca. 1762
Lent by Mr. and Mrs. A. Herenroth, New York

erally ignored by the West; prejudice has obscured the West's view of Russian art. Until some fifty years ago, the West considered Russian history to begin with Peter the Great, Russian literature with the writers Tolstoy and Dostoyevsky, and Russian music with Tchaikovsky. The interest in Russia's plastic genius arose only with the development of decorative painting in the first decade of this century, such as Diaghilev's brilliant productions of opera and ballet in Paris. Yet, Russian painting, although at some moments the handmaiden of literature, has made its own contribution to world culture; and artists — known and unknown — have created values which have permanent artistic significance.

Failure to appreciate Russian art was true not only of the West. In 1902, Alexander Benois, the Russian artist and art-historian, wrote in his "History of Painting": Is there in Russia a lack of talent in the pictorial arts, which some believe is caused by Russia's geographical situation — its seemingly monotonous and vast expanses that do not stimulate the imagination, or is it the historical factor — the centuries-long state of slavery of the lower classes — that prevented the full development of Russian talent?" Benois categorically asserts the presence of Russian talent in painting and lists names of painters who in his estimation deserve attention. He further comments on why Russian painting was not properly appreciated by the Russians themselves: "Is it not due to the conflict...followed by the laziness and apathy ("Oblomovshchina") caused by the alienation from the soil...which exists between the deeply-rooted folk-life and the imported culture which we still accept so painfully without being able to feel comfortable with it after 200 years? There is still the same misunderstanding between the Russian people and Russian art, the same as 200 years ago when, along with caftans and wigs, Peter the Great imported Dutch and German paintings and Italian statues. How would it have been possible for people so suddenly to love different allegories, strange gods, saints and angels, since until then they were obliged to hate all of this?"[1]

Thus, according to some conceptions both Russian and foreign, Peter the Great's reforms harshly interrupted the development of an independent Russian culture, by encouraging the entry into Russia of foreign influences. It is from then on that Russian art lost its national character and subjugated itself to Western European examples. This point of view lasted for a long time.

In this context, it may be of interest to quote a statement of Konstantin S. Aksakov, the Slavophile critic of the first half of the nineteenth century: "Russia is an absolutely original country, quite unlike European states and institutions. Those who would seek historical standards by which to judge Russia are greatly mistaken." These words point out the futility of an attempt to compare that which is Russian with that which is Western; the issue of comparison of culture in general or of painting in particular was either ignored or denounced.

Beginning with the nineteenth century, art critics of the West characterized Russian painting

DIMITRI G. LEVITSKI. *Portrait of Leonidoff, Ambassador to the Court of Egypt.* Undated
Lent by Mr. and Mrs. André Harley, New York

ALEXEI G. VENETSIANOV. *Girl.* Undated
Lent by Mr. George Riabov, New York

as absolutely dependent on the art of Europe. Since many of the Russian art historians of the pre-World War I period adhered to this point of view, then it is more obvious why foreign scholars were predisposed to share the same opinions.

Contrary to what one may think, a considerable number of books on Russian painting of the eighteenth through twentieth centuries have been written within the last fifty years. There exist a great number of statements about Russian art by French, German and English scholars. However, most of the material written in the beginning of the century is only of insignificant interest because it adopts the information and evaluations of Russian sources, chiefly Benois. Only on rare occasions were foreign authors able to make fresh and original observations about Russian art.

In Denis Roche, a French expert on Russian art who in 1904 wrote a monograph on the eighteenth-century portraitist, D. G. Levitsky,[2] Russian painting found an apt critic. Roche did claim that Levitsky gained the ability to portray the human figure and to reveal the human face from the French. However, he also says that Levitsky was a painter who, thanks to his extraordinary talent, laid the foundations for the development of Russian painting. It is even more important to add that Roche accused the Russians of failure to acquaint the West with the great talent of Levitsky.

All of the books, beginning with the French Denis Roche and Louis Reau,[3] the English Rosa Newmarch,[4] the American George Heard Hamilton,[5] and the Germans Oskar Wulff[6] and Fritz Nemitz,[7] affirm the opinion that Russian artists of the eighteenth century can stand comparison with their contemporaries in the West, although they persist in stating that the expression of Russian talent was almost exclusively French in inspiration and that it is not easy to find Russian traits in Russian painting during this period. The same regrettable attitude applied to the analysis of Russian art of the nineteenth century.

A different opinion by a foreign art historian is expressed by Tamara Talbot Rice who has given credit where it is due; for instance, when evaluating the talent of Levitsky, she wrote: "It is unfortunate that Catherine (the Great) never sat for Dimitri Levitsky...who can be termed the Gainsborough of Russian art...He chose to paint portraits in the grand manner, yet none of these is in any sense an academic picture; each is embued with vitality, and the majority stand out both as works of art and as fascinating records of the personality and idiosyncracies of the great personages of his day."[8] It is a remarkable fact that the majority of the multi-volume series on the art of the world, which were published in the different countries of the West within the first half of the century, almost completely ignore Russian painting.

Reviews of Russian painting started to appear in the West in connection with a number of exhibitions organized in the nineteen-twenties and early thirties:

"Exhibition of Russian Painting and Sculpture", Brooklyn Museum, New York, 1923

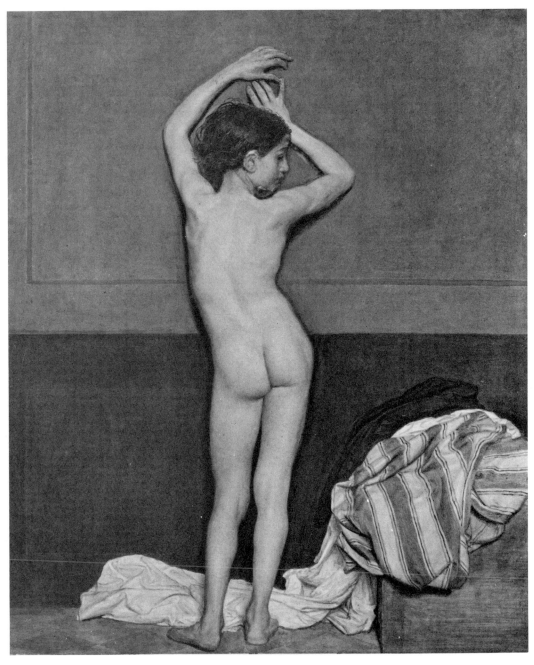

ALEXANDER A. IVANOV.   *Study of a Nude Boy for the Painting "Christ Before the People".*   Undated
Lent by Mr. and Mrs. Boris Pregel, New York

12

IVAN K. AIVAZOVSKY.   *Sunset.*   1876
Lent by Mr. Igor Sobin, Whitestone, New York

(Russian art of the nineteen-twenties).

"Art Russe Ancien et Moderne", Palais des Beaux-Arts, Bruxelles, 1928.

"Exhibition of Contemporary Art of Soviet Russia", Grand Central Palace, New York, 1929.

"Exposition d'Art Russe (de 1906 à 1932)", Galerie "La Renaissance", Paris, 1932.

"Exhibition of Russian Art", Belgrave Square, London, 1935.

"Five Hundred Years of Russian Art", The Gould House Galleries, Gimbel Brothers, New York, late 1940's.

Most of these exhibitions were composed of works of art in private collections, mainly those of Russians living abroad, while only an insignificant number of works came from Russian and non-Russian museums.

In connection with the exhibition held in London in 1935, D. Talbot Rice published a book containing a series of articles on different aspects of Russian art, written mostly by Russian emigrés.[9] These essays are interesting in that they offer the first discussions outside of Russia of the reasons for the ignorance of Russian art in the West. A. Polovtsev in his essay entitled "A Historical Survey" explains that Russians themselves, beginning with the epoch of Peter the Great, underestimated their own art and exaggerated the value of all foreign art.

Alexander Benois in his essay on Russian art of the eighteenth century turned back to the theme which preoccupied him some thirty years earlier. In restating the issue of the under-rating of Russian art, he suggested a different reason for the neglect. In contrast to Polovtsev, he no longer blamed the Russians but suggested that the West was responsible for the general indifference to Russian art. According to Benois there existed on the part of Western observors a certain preconception, which led them to expect from all things Russian a single quality — an entertaining but rather barbarous exoticism. If products of Russian culture were not reminiscent of the style of the cossacks or gypsies, such as the Polovtsian dances of Borodin's "Prince Igor", then the West has been unwilling to regard them as innately Russian rather than mere imitations of other cultures.

During the last ten years, a series of exhibitions of Russian and Soviet art organized by the Soviet Union has taken place outside of Russia — in 1957 in Warsaw[10] and Peking,[11] in 1959 in London[12] and New York,[13] in 1960 in Paris,[14] Montreal, Ottawa, and Toronto,[15] and in 1963 in New York.[16] These exhibitions were seen by many and reviewed by many critics. The English critic John Russell, reviewing the exhibition at the Royal Academy in 1959, made some interesting and intelligent observations. He is of the opinion that Russian painters have always been confident of their own powers without feeling a sense of competition with the icon painters of the past or the great masters of the West. Characterizing the unique position of art in Russia, Russell observed: "In Russia itself, paintings were never seen in

ILYA REPIN. *Greetings in the Church after the Wedding.* 1894
Lent by Mr. Peter Tretyakoff, New York

VLADIMIR Y. MAKOVSKY. *Family Scene.* 1888
Lent by Mr. Ira Spanierman, New York

16

KARL P. BRYULLOV.   *Portrait of Countess Samoilova.*   Undated
Lent by Dr. Armand Hammer, New York

exquisite isolation: icons were installed on a screen which could take as many as fifty or sixty; canvasses hang three and four deep in the museums . . . At a gallery like the Tretyakov in Moscow, the visitor is struck . . . by two things: the superabundance of work on view, and the degree to which Russian visitors *live* the pictures before them . . . the intensity of response goes far beyond any consideration of esthetics."[17] Russell criticized the installation of the London exhibition for its isolation of the paintings "as if they were Chardins or Vermeers" and its consequent failure to communicate the sympathy for great story-telling which their native settings do.

However, none of the above-mentioned exhibitions contained examples of Russian contributions to the modern movements of world art. According to the criteria of Socialist Realism which have prevailed in Soviet Russia for some decades, the only acceptable modern forms are those which stress the universal emotions as felt and expressed by the common people. Thus one was not able to see in these exhibitions works by such artists as Kandinsky, Tatlin, Malevich, Chagall, and many others who were considered to have departed from realism in the direction of excessive formalism. The contribution of these Russian innovators,[18] however, is of the greatest importance to the development of modern art in the West; therefore their work is included in this survey in order that they may be viewed as a link in the process of reconsideration of values which is part of the history of Russian art.

More fortunate in the general recognition of its universal value was Russian icon painting. The intrinsic beauty of icons was disclosed only at the turn of the century, when due to the combined efforts of art scholars, painters and restorers, the crudely applied coats of overpaint were removed from the original paintings. Russian icons came gloriously alive, and once again, the beauty of line and color could move the viewer esthetically and spiritually. Beginning with 1913 when the most interesting of the old icons were exhibited in Russia, and afterwards in 1929-30 in Germany, Great Britain and the United States, Russian icon painting won world renown. It has since been studied in many countries, with many books and albums appearing on the subject. To mention a few: *The Russian Icon,* by N. P. Kondakov in 1927, and *The Meaning of Icons* by Leonid Ouspensky and Vladimir Lossky in 1952. UNESCO has made important contributions to the literature on icon-painting; in 1958 *Early Russian Icons* was published by V. N. Lazarev in the U.S.S.R.; Konrad Onash's *Icons* appeared in 1961; and the *Catalogue of Ancient Russian Painting* of the Tretyakov Gallery Collection was published in two volumes in 1963.

The very considerable work and study required to restore and preserve icons brought their 800 year-old history to light. By now scholars have established not only the main periods of development but also the characteristics of the various schools. The early phase of ancient Russian painting, since the adoption of Christianity in the tenth century, stems from Byzantium. But the seeds of Greek art that were planted in Russian soil yielded unique fruit. The Russian

VASILY I. SURIKOV. *Portrait of Repin.* 1882
Lent by Mr. and Mrs. Andrei Sedych, New York

18

spirit and cultural tradition acted as a catalyst that influenced the most noted Byzantine masters working in the country.

From the time of its origin in the 11th century down to the 18th century, the art of the icon, which means picture in Greek, adhered to a traditional style which can be compared to the Romanesque style of the West. A sharp contrast between Russian and Western painting set in with the rise of the Gothic style in the West. In the succeeding centuries the contrast deepened until it attained that complete cleavage which can be strikingly illustrated by a comparison of paintings by Jan van Eyck with the contemporary Andrey Rublev.

The subject matter of icons has always reflected religious doctrine. The Council at Nicaea in 843 established the image of the Divinity. Since the image, no less than scripture, bears witness to the great act of salvation by representing the human figure as sanctified by the Incarnation, it was held to be as sacred as scripture. But the image could only maintain its position as sacred by remaining as changeless as scripture. No emphasis was permitted on the corporeality of earthly things, even by effect of light and shade. No personal or emotional content could be introduced. However, just as a priest of God officiates before the altar in accordance with his character and circumstances, so the artist recreated a religious image according to his character and talent. The anonymity of authorship of most of the Russian icons is to be explained by the attitude of humility of the Russian icon painters, who regarded their work as a sacred contribution to the glorification of God. It was only in the seventeenth century that signatures on the reverse or on the margin were attached.

Theophanes the Greek (ca. 1330-1405) was an artist of great talent and a significant figure in the development of fifteenth-century Russian art. His Novgorod and Moscow works strongly influenced Russian painters, most notably *Andrey Rublev* (ca. 1360-1430), whose icons gave exquisite expression to his religious view of the world. His "Trinity", acknowledged a masterpiece by connoisseurs and art scholars, is a rhythmic flow of harmonious movement and understated colors, an expression of calm bliss and radiant joy. The Russian N. P. Kondakov felt that Rublev was inferior to the Italians. The American scholar Alfred H. Barr, Jr., wrote: "He is certainly more limited. But is there any painting of Fra Angelico's or even of Sassetta's that can approach the detached authority of the "Trinity"? Beside this masterpiece, their work seems obvious, occasionally trivial, or even banal."[19]

In the second half of the fifteenth century, *Dionysius* (ca. 1440-1502) carried on the Rublev tradition. He introduced a festive note in his paintings which caught the fancy of the court of the Moscow principality. Dionysius' icons are characterized by refined and elegant brushwork and a radiant glow of unearthly phosphorescence.

Sixteenth-century Russian icon painting resembles late Gothic art of the West a few centuries earlier with its scholastic allegories, sophisticated didacticism, and complexity of subject. From the moment that the Russian icon became the medium for theological ideas,

KONSTANTIN A. KOROVIN.   *Paris on a Rainy Night.*   1939
Lent by Mr. and Mrs. Jacques Garvin, New York

VALENTIN A. SEROV. *Portrait of a Boy.* Undated
Lent by Mr. George Riabov, New York

the purely artistic quality diminished: the colors acquired muddy and dim tones and the irreproachable rhythm and harmony of lines weakened.

In the seventeenth century, bright colors, minute compositions and linear mannerisms predominated. The icons are miniaturistic in scale; the figures are elegant and slender in proportion. These are lovely and highly precious objects, even if they are not great works of art. Certain of the icons have inscriptions stating that they were made for the wealthy Stroganov family. *Procopius Chirin* and *Istoma Savin* are the foremost painters of this school.

It was not until the end of the seventeenth century, when Western ideas were introduced, that Russian art broke its bondage to the old Byzantine tradition. *Simon Ushakov's* art was a mixture of Byzantine, Western and Russian characteristics, but he introduced realism into icon painting, a style that would be imitated until the end of the nineteenth century. The great tradition of religious icon painting came to an end in the late seventeenth century. However, it is still able to exercise a magical spell by its rhythmic sense, harmonious composition, ethereal monumentality, and an inspired message divined in terms of artistic beauty.

Since the fifteenth century, "riza" — ornamented embossed metal casings mounted with precious stones, which reveal only hands and faces of the painted images — have become more and more popular. "Basma" covers only the edges of the icons; "aklad" conceals everything except for the figures.

The eighteenth century was the period in which the old canons of icon painting were deliberately broken. Painting started to move towards realistic representation; and portrait painting, first on wood and later on canvas, began to flourish. Prior to this time, portrait painting was rare and incidental. Neither Rublev nor Dionysius ever tried it. Only in the seventeenth century appeared what was termed "person-painting" — for the most part portraits of the czars and members of their families, statesmen and church dignitaries. These still echoed very closely all the stylistic elements of icon painting — the ornamental style, lack of perspective, and the meticulous reproduction of minute details, especially of rich costumes and vestments.

The new portrait painting began with Peter the Great (1682-1725), who opened a "window on Europe" for himself and his country. In place of the ancient Russian ideal of the religious order, the vigorous, energetic and strong man of history came to the fore, and thus began the history of secular painting in Russia. Peter the Great sent his artists abroad to Paris, Rome and Holland to study; he also brought to Russia many European artists, among them Lampi, Tannauer, etc.

The "person-painting" tradition persisted for some decades of the eighteenth century, as is evident in the portrait of "Catherine II in Mourning for Elizabeth" by *Evgraf P. Chemesov*. In the 1730's the harsh attitude of Empress Anna Leopoldovna somewhat retarded the development of Russian portraiture. Nevertheless the traditions born of the heroic times of

LEV. BAKST.   *Turk with Scimitar.*   1921
Lent by Mr. and Mrs. Boris Pregel, New York

23

FILIP A. MALYAVIN.   *Girls.*   Undated
Lent by Mr. George Riabov, New York

Peter the Great were continued by *Aleksey P. Antropov* (1716-1795), a highly original portraitist and the teacher of Levitsky, Russia's most famous eighteenth-century portrait painter. When *Dimitri G. Levitsky* (1735-1822) exhibited a collection of his portraits in 1770, the impression they made on his contemporaries was tremendous. This master of formal and informal painting was known all over Europe; thus Diderot preferred Levitsky's portrait of himself to all others. A noted contemporary was *Nikolay I. Argunov* (1771-1829).

An important part in the development of Russian art was played by the Academy of Fine Arts, founded in St. Petersburg in 1757, which helped to cultivate an appreciation of art in the nation. The paintings produced by graduates of that time are mostly allegorical representations, glorifying the activities of the court.

The last of the great eighteenth-century Russian portraitists was *Vladimir L. Borovikovsky* (1757-1825). He rightly belongs to the generation linking the art of the eighteenth and nineteenth centuries. His was a time when sentimentality was the vogue, and many of its conventions are to be found in his pictures. His portraits have a rhythm and soft outline well-suited to the wistful and pensive faces of his beautiful sitters. Borovikovsky's portraits are an example of his mastery of all the elements of typical eighteenth-century painting, the crowning achievement of the Russian school of formal, ceremonial portraiture.

Graphic art had begun in the sixteenth century in Russia. Woodcuts and block prints were used by the early Russian printers as book illustrations. Either in black and white or colored by hand, woodcuts were mainly outline drawings. The Old and New Testament illustrations in this exhibition illustrate the unification of the formal Byzantine tradition of icon painting and the European style of painting.

The first printing press began operation in Moscow in 1764. The mass-produced prints, known as "lubki", became popular in the eighteenth century and from then on found a permanent market throughout Russia. They were still produced during the first World War to answer the demand of the lower classes for pictorial matter closer to ordinary life than icon painting.

The art of the "lubki" is very complex in subject matter and execution. Incidents from history, both sacred and secular; scenes of the life of the people; bitingly satirical sayings, proverbs, and songs; stark realism and vivid fantasy are illustrated in gloriously harmonious colors; they were hand-colored by the peasants during the long winter nights. Pre-Christian myths of Slavic ancestry seem to have been of influence on this folk art,[20] which in turn influenced the work of such painters as Chagall and Malevich.

The Bible pictures of Adam and Eve, cut on wood in 1696 by *Vasily Koren* from designs by the master Grigoriy, indicate the great talent of this master of woodcuts.

Beside the "lubki", Russian folk art manifested itself through miniatures painted on lac-

LUBOK *(folk print)*
Lent by Mr. Alexander Liberman, New York

26

ALEXANDER BENOIS.   *View of the Chapel at Tsarskoye Selo.*   Undated
Lent by Mr. and Mrs. Jacques Garvin, New York

NICHOLAS ROERICH. *Stage Design for "The Rites of Spring": Dancers in Bearskins.* Undated
Lent by the Nicholas Roerich Museum, New York

quered surfaces of papier-maché in the village of Palekh. In the seventeenth century peasants of the village of Palekh, near Moscow, started to apply their icon technique to secular subjects. This village commune of Palekh, an academy of folk art, continues at the present to maintain the traditional elaborate, decorative style and strictly formal compositions. The exhibited lacquered box executed in Palekh in 1927 shows a young man at a well attended by two women — a formal theme drawn from a representation of Christ with Martha and Mary.[21]

Russia gave the world Pushkin, the greatest Russian poet and the symbol of his country's cultural flourishing during the early decades of the nineteenth century. Russian painting of the period produced no figure of comparable stature, but it did reflect Russia's effervescent spiritual growth.

Orest A. Kiprensky (1782-1836), an outstanding portrait painter, executed his paintings in a romantic, but nevertheless deeply realistic, style. Russia is indebted to him for the finest portraits of Pushkin and Zhukovsky among others. Kiprensky's talent was acknowledged in Europe. He was the first Russian painter to receive a commission from the Uffizi Gallery in Florence for a self-portrait, an honor accorded only the most celebrated masters.

Silvester F. Shchedrin (1791-1830) was an outstanding landscape painter of the emerging school of realism. Charmed by the landscapes of Italy, his favorite subject, he painted many scenes of Rome and Naples. His canvases, radiant with a sense of light and air, express a joyful serenity which echoes the harmonious feeling for nature of Pushkin's poetry.

Genre painting was also characteristic of the Pushkin period. *Aleksey G. Venetsianov* (1780-1847), who began as a portraitist in the eighteen-twenties, later turned to the depiction of Russian life and customs. He was the first Russian painter to find esthetic and ethical values in everyday subjects, which until then had been considered unworthy of an artist's consideration but subsequently became the dominant theme of Russian nineteenth-century painting.

Karl P. Bryullov (1798-1852) established his reputation at home and abroad with his "Last Day of Pompeii", which was praised by Walter Scott and inspired Bulwer-Lytton's novel. He was also a brilliant portrait-painter. Bryullov's talent was inhibited by the academic trend, but not to the degree that his individuality or his feeling for the nature of man were stultified.

The realistic trend gradually became part of the Russian academic tradition. This was especially evident in the work of *Alexander A. Ivanov* (1806-1858). For some twenty years he worked on his "Christ Appears to the People." It has been said that in this religious canvas Ivanov painted a vision of a universal harmony of free mankind, his conception of the elevated and the sublime united with the earthly and the human. In preparation for the painting, Ivanov made more than six hundred studies for the human figure which are small masterpieces in themselves.

Pavel A. Fedotov (1815-1852), who is considered the founder of the Russian school of critical realism, turned his eyes toward the world around him. Fedotov's art derided the evils of the social system and revealed a profound sympathy for human suffering, approaching Gogol and Dostoevsky in its compassion.

Ivan N. Kramskoy (1837-1887) had an important influence on painting, not because of his artistic talent but through his organizational ability. In 1863, he became a leader of a movement toward realism among young painters, who refused to participate in their graduation examinations upon proscribed allegorical subjects and demanded the right of individual choice. When they were refused, this group of thirteen resigned and organized their own workshop.

In 1872, the year of the first great exhibition of Impressionists in France, Kramskoy organized the Society of Travelling Exhibitions *(Obshchestvo Peredvizhnikov)* in direct protest against the Academy. The first signs of revolt emerged in a manifesto by Nikolay Tchernyshevsky (1828-1889), "The Esthetic Relationship Between Art and Reality" (1855), in which the author specified a definite social purpose for art. He declared the superiority of reality to its imitation. From this it followed that subject and impression were more important than form, and that in the interests of social order the choice of subject is all important. Realism was to the "Peredvizhniki" a means to an end: to bring art to the people and to inspire and enlighten them. They attached far more importance to the moral and literary aspect of art than to esthetics. For more than two decades this group dominated the scene. The chief painters of the movement were Kramskoy, Repin, Savrasov, Perov, Surikov, and Makovsky.

Ilya E. Repin (1844-1930) was perhaps the most gifted of the "Peredvizhniki" and best expressed the movement's spirit. In his best known paintings: "The Volga Burlaks" (1873), "Religious Procession in Kursk Province" (1877-1883), "Unexpected" (1884), "Ivan the Terrible Kills his Son" (1885), "Zaporozhye Cossacks Writing a letter to the Turkish Sultan" (1890-91), he established himself as a master of literal detailed realism which sometimes attains epic proportions. Among his best works are his portraits of cossacks, whom he knew intimately. His art has had a direct influence on Socialist Realism of the present.

In the landscapes as in the genre scenes of the "Peredvizhniki", the common and humble are emphasized in deliberate contrast to the ostentation of salon and academic painting. This is apparent in the paintings by *Ivan I. Shishkin* (1832-98) of forests and grainfields.

Arkhip I. Kuindzhi (1842-1910) presented the Russian landscape in ecstatic and lyric tones with intense light and burning colors.

Vladimir E. Makovsky (1846-1920) painted portraits and genre scenes that dealt with the life of the middle and lower classes of his day. Many of the Soviet artists have been influenced by his work.

Vasily D. Polenov (1844-1927) was a master of landscape and an excellent colorist. As a

MSTISLAV V. DOBOUJINSKY. *"The City Visions: Labor"*. Undated
Lent by Mr. Vsevolod Doboujinsky, Brooklyn, New York

KASIMIR MALEVICH. *Argentine Polka.* 1905
Lent by Mr. Joachim Aberbach, Sands Point, New York

ISAAK K. LEVITAN.   *Still Waters.*   Undated
Lent by Mr. George Riabov, New York

SAVELY A. SORIN.   *Portrait of Maxim Gorki.*   Undated
Lent by the M. H. de Young Memorial Museum, San Francisco

result of his journey to the East, he produced a cycle of paintings of the life of Christ.

Vasily V. Vereshchagin (1842-1904) was a painter of battle scenes who portrayed his horror of war; however, his ideological convictions destroyed his art.

Sergey A. Vinogradov (1869-1938) was a plein-airist who painted genre pictures in an impressionistic manner.

Maksimilian A. Voloshin (1837-1931) was a symbolist and a mystic who painted melancholy views of the Crimea in delicate watercolors, reminiscent of Japanese art.

Apolinari M. Vasnetsov (1856-1933) was interested in the popular history of the past, especially in the archeological reconstruction of old Moscow of the pre-Peter the First era.

An orthodox religious and humanist painter, *Mikhail V. Nesterov* (1862-1942) painted lyrical scenes of Russian landscapes with churches, monks and saints in the foreground.

More nationalistic than religious was *Vasili I. Surikov* (1848-1916) who broke with the sentimental, humanitarian ideals of the "Peredvizhniki" and recreated scenes from the history of Russia in brilliant but sombre peasant colors.

At the time when the realist painters were in vogue, a new movement entered Russia from France. Impressionism was welcomed by younger artists who were aware of current French painting and excited by the color discoveries of Monet and Pissarro. The work of the doctrinaire Russian Impressionists was devoted to landscape painting of actual out-of-doors scenes and actual people. Among the early leaders of Impressionism was *Valentin A. Serov* (1865-1911), an outstanding portrait painter, whose virtuosity in drawing and painting permitted him to express the most essential characteristics of his models in a terse style.

Isaak K. Levitan (1861-1900) was the greatest of Russian landscape painters. His profoundly native landscapes give an expression of the Russian sense of "Mother Russia".

Mikhail A. Vrubel (1856-1900) was the best of the fantastic Impressionists. His complex representations of fantastic visions are bold in brushwork and beautiful in color.

Victor E. Borisov-Musatov (1870-1905) recreated the life of the Russian manor of the 1830's, portraying in poetic nuances of color the human being as possessing visionary and mysterious qualities.

Konstantin A. Somov (1869-1939) was an impressionistic painter of landscapes and intimate scenes reminiscent of eighteenth-century France, executed mostly in brilliant water colors. He was also known as a designer and portrait painter.

Boris M. Kustodiev (1878-1927) painted idealized versions of the life of the provinces, especially of the merchant class, as well as portraits, genre and landscapes.

In the first years of the twentieth century, the main line of Russian Impressionism followed Vrubel in deserting the natural world. Painting became concerned with a decorative linearism

NATHALIE GONTCHAROVA.　*Stage Design: "The City"*.　Undated
Lent by Mrs. V. N. Bashkiroff, New Preston, Connecticut

MIKHAIL F. LARIONOV. *Composition.* Undated
Lent by Mr. and Mrs. Boris Pregel, New York

ALEXEI JAWLENSKY. *Infanta.* 1912-1913
Lent by Mr. and Mrs. Serge Sabarsky, Courtesy of Leonard Hutton Galleries, New York

which had a decisive influence on design for the theatre — especially in the settings for the Russian ballet, which was making its first grand tour of Europe. Most of these painters were associated with the "World of Art" group, which was organized as a protest against the "Peredvizhniki" in St. Petersburg in 1890 and originally included both the fantastic and realistic Impressionists. *Serge P. Diaghilev* (1872-1929), the great Russian impressario, patron of the arts and originator of the "World of Art", wrote: "I want to revise Russian painting, cleanse it and bring it to the notice of the West — make it big and known."

Alexander N. Benois (1870-1960), writer and art critic, was the leader of the "World of Art" movement and one of the editors of the art magazine published under the same title. "Art for art's sake" was the slogan of the whole group, and they all stood for interpretation rather than imitation of nature. As opposed to the "Peredvizhniki", the "World of Art" was strictly without political motivation. "The reactions of art to earthly difficulties are not worthy of the Soul of the Divinity. The only function of art is pleasure, its only instrument beauty."[22]

These thoughts about beauty and divine inspiration were very typical of the period, in Russia as in the West. Admiration of France of the Rococo period and of old Russia inspired the highly stylized paintings by the "World of Art" members: Alexander N. Benois, Konstantin A. Somov, Lev S. Bakst, Yevgeny Y. Lanceret, Mstislav V. Doboujinsky, Nikolay K. Roerich, Konstantin A. Korovin, Alexander Y. Golovin, Ivan Y. Bilibin, etc. This new decorative art of the "World of Art" movement, centered around Savva I. Mamontov in St. Petersburg and the estate of Abramtsevo near Moscow, had an important influence on the popular arts, book illustration, mural painting, and chiefly the ballet, specifically that connected with Diaghilev. Herbert Read wrote in 1963: "Diaghilev ballets, from 1909 onwards, were the visible and aggressive embodiment of the avant-garde; without them the mainbody of the modern movement would have been delayed for decades."[23]

Post-impressionism, Fauvism, and Cubism reached Russia almost simultaneously with their appearance in Western Europe. Many Russian artists were living in the West, and the extraordinary collections of modern art brought to Russia by the merchants Ivan Morozov and Sergey Shchukin acquainted the artists at home with the new advances. Some Russian artists living in France came under the influence of primitive art; others who were in contact with Fauves and the early Expressionists in Germany became interested in forms and colors that did not imitate nature.

The first decade of the twentieth century was characterized by the number of small groups pursuing individual paths in the general direction of modernism. Some painters were called the Primitivists, many of whom later formed various opposing groups: "The Jack of Diamonds," "The Blue Rose," "The Donkey Tail," etc. During the first World War, as well as during and after the Revolution of 1917, new movements regularly came into being: the

SERGEY SUDEYKIN. *Costume Design for a Clown.* Undated
Lent by Mr. Paul Fekula, Elmhurst, New York

"Imagists", the "Rayonnists", the "Suprematists", and the "Constructivists".

One of the most gifted of the "Primitivists" is *Marc Chagall* (1889-), who, using motifs from Jewish and Russian folklore and the life of his native Vitebsk, created a naive and fantastic world, a vision of poetic beauty, in which Cubist elements are fused with folk art color and Expressionist mood. "My pictures are not literature. They are painted arrangements of inner images that obsess me."

Mikhail F. Larionov (1881-1964) and his wife *Nathalie S. Gontcharova* (1881-1962) developed the concept of Rayonnism. Under the influence of Signac and Analytic Cubism, they represented landscapes and figures in color patterns based on the form of sheaves and ray-lines. Parallel with Kandinsky's abstract Expressionism, the Rayonnism of Larionov and Gontcharova significantly influenced the advance of purely abstract painting.

Vasily V. Kandinsky (1866-1944) developed further the color discoveries of the Fauves into a new plastic language of line and color without obvious subject matter. He is generally regarded as the creator of the first purely abstract paintings in 1910. In 1910 Kandinsky wrote in the manuscript of his book "The Spiritual in Art" (published in 1912): "The music of abstract color areas should be sufficient to carry the inner music of things to which man's soul responds." Kandinsky's painting is "the project of a new world"; using new tools, he created pictorial allegories, just as Rublev did in his "Trinity" — "symbols that belong on the altars of the coming spiritual religion," as Franz Marc put it.

Alexei von Jawlensky (1864-1941), influenced by Kandinsky, Matisse and the brilliant color of Russian folk art, created paintings of mystical meditation. By simplifying the contours, tying them firmly to the surface and enhancing the colors, he arrived at the modern icon.

Another original painter, *Kasimir S. Malevich* (1878-1935) evolved the theory which he called Suprematism. He sent his famous canvas "White on White" to a big Moscow exhibition in 1919. This painting, whose basic principles are economy in the plastic means, rhythm of lines and planes, and the universal relationship achieved through primary color and elementary geometric forms, remains the best demonstration of Suprematism. Malevich declared that Suprematism means "the supremacy of pure feeling or perception in the pictorial arts." The square on the pure surface, "an experience of the non-objective", became the starting point of absolute painting.

Vladimir E. Tatlin (1885-1953), the great advocate of Constructivism, proclaimed the death of easel painting and the birth of a new art which found a model for its rhythm, construction and logic in the machine. Constructivist works were not reproductions of things, but were themselves "organized beauty" with an esthetic validity as such. Tatlin found no material unworthy of use for art; glass, wood and metals were employed to express the emotions evoked by science and technical progress.

El Lissitzky (1890-1941) is the Constructivist best known outside of Russia. Under the

BORIS D. GRIGORIEV. *Portrait of a Man.* Undated
Lent by Mr. George Riabov, New York

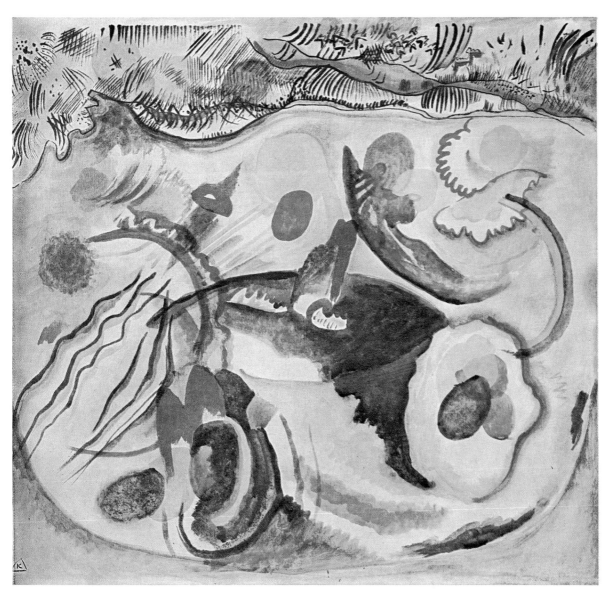

VASILY V. KANDINSKY. *Theme of the Deluge and the Last Judgement.* 1913
Lent by the Leonard Galleries, New York

ALEXANDER T. YAKOVLEV. *Head of a Mongol.* 1931
Lent by Mr. George Riabov, New York

influence of Malevich's perspective constructions, he declared that the purpose of art is not to beautify but to transform and organize life, until life and art merge. His works, compositions based on stereometric elements — "prouns" as he called them, are a mutation of painting and architectural ornament. For him works of art were not to exist as separate objects but to become part of the total environment.

Alexander M. Rodchenko (1891-1956), in love with linear figurations, constructed mathematically geometrical compositions which attained high quality as decorative designs.

After the Revolution of 1917, many Russian painters achieved their reputations outside of their native land, some eventually returning to Russia.

The stage and costume designs of *Lev S. Bakst* (1866-1924) have an affinity with Persian miniatures in their harmony of exquisite colors and delicately wrought lines.

Alexander N. Benois (1870-1960) advocated the revolutionary creed of a total collaboration between composer, dancer, painter and choreographer. He was able to mirror in his designs the spirit of any given time and place. His watercolors show his deep love for Russia of the past.

Alexander Y. Golovin (1864-1930) was less refined as a stage designer than Bakst, but he was more Russian in flavor, more dramatic and forceful.

Nathalie Gontcharova produced some of the most outstanding stage designs, which are characterized by bold, simplified outlines and harmonious colors.

Mikhail Larionov was a most inventive stage designer, who used primitivistic and bizarre forms to produce striking effects.

David D. Burliuk (1882-1967), one of the Fauves of Russia, was among the first propagators of modern art. He painted in a primitive, mystical style with a literary folk-art approach.

Konstantin A. Korovin (1861-1939), the Russian Impressionist, painted brilliant views of Paris while thinking longingly of Russia.

Vasily I. Shukhaev (1887-), a master of costume and stage designs, also painted interesting landscapes with an essential honesty of visual representation.

Alexander E. Yakovlev (1887-1938) was a masterful draughtsman whose sanguine drawings of people encountered on his extensive travels attain the expressiveness of icon painting.

Sergey Y. Sudeykin (1882-1946), an excellent colorist of great musical sense and imagination, recreated Russia's picturesque nineteenth century.

Roman (Robert) R. Falk (1886-1958), profoundly influenced by Matisse and Cezanne, member of the Moscow "Knave of Diamonds" group, painted poetic still-lifes and landscapes.

Savely A. Sorin (1878-1953) received wide recognition for his sensitive psychological interpretation of people in a style of linear beauty and subtle color.

Boris D. Grigoriev (1886-1939) provided a strange, apocalyptic vision, a nostalgic memory

OSCAR RABIN. *City with Moons.* 1962
Lent by the Grosvenor Gallery, New York

of Russia in his series of paintings entitled "Visages Russes," done in a remarkable neo-Cubist style.

Ivan Y. Bilibin (1876-1942) was influenced by popular art and made some beautiful illustrations of Russian fairy tales, in addition to theatrical scenery.

Mstislav V. Doboujinsky (1875-1957) was a stage designer true to Russian folklore and an important book-illustrator. His style is distinguished by clarity of outline and a subtle simplicity of technique.

Filip A. Malyavin (1869-1939) painted with a loose, impressionistic brushstroke; his chief subjects were broad-cheeked Russian village women and girls in colorful garments.

Leonid O. Pasternak (1862-1917) painted, in an impressionistic manner, subtle portraits of Tolstoy, Chaliapine and members of his own family.

Sergey V. Tchekhonin (1878-1936) is known for his beautiful line drawings.

George K. Lukomsky, an architect and painter of architecture, depicted the beauty of the buildings of Kiev, St. Petersburg and its vicinity, in an exacting but pictorially interesting manner.

In the early days of the Russian Revolution of 1917, painting was instantly brought into the service of the new regime. Vladimir I. Lenin said: "Art belongs to the people. It must have its deepest roots in the broad masses of the workers. It must be understood and loved by them and no others." However, both the "Right" and the "Left" continued to paint according to their own standards. Nevertheless the Leftists were criticized by the masses; and with the introduction of the New Economic Policy, realism found its way back. The nineteenth-century tradition of academic realism was considered to be more useful to the new state than Futurism, Constructivism, Suprematism and the other "isms."

In 1930, the Soviet government announced that "all the workers of the Soviet Union, building socialism with revolutionary enthusiasm, having achieved gigantic successes in realizing the five-year plan, must strike a hatchet at all efforts to restore the bourgeois system... There can be no apolitical attitude in science and art. One who is not an ally of the proletariat is his enemy."

In 1932, the dogma of Socialist Realism was proclaimed by *Pravda,* and the formation of the Union of Soviet Artists was ordered by the Central Committee of the Communist party. Nikita Khrushchev explained the ideals of Socialist Realism in his speech at a meeting in the Kremlin on March 8, 1963: "Our people need a militant revoluntionary art. Soviet literature and art are called upon to reproduce in vivid artistic imagery the great and heroic epoch of communist construction, to depict truthfully the assertion and victory of the new communist relations in our life. The artist must be able to see the positive things and to rejoice at them, for they make up the essence of our reality; he must support these things but, at the same time, of course, must not overlook the negative phenomena and all that interferes with

NATHALIE GONTCHAROVA. *Costume Design for "Le Coq d'Or": A Man.* 1914
Lent by Mr. George Riabov, New York

the rise of the new life."

As stated previously, it is with a deep-felt sense of inadequacy that certain phases of Russian painting are represented in this survey. There are no works available of Isaac J. Brodsky, Igor E. Grabar, Alexander N. Gerasimov, Boris V. Ioganson, Sergey Malyatin, G. Ryazhsky, A. Pakhomov, N. Zhukov, A. Plastov, T. Gaponenko, and many others that would illustrate the artistic expression of the Socialist Realists.

Recently some artists have found new directions in art which they themselves feel are not definitively marked out. The Russian art critic of the magazine *Soviet Life,* Yuri Ovsyannikov, wrote in an article entitled "Introducing Five Young Painters": "They are seekers and will remain seekers, learning through trial and error, so that they may again and again embark on what seems the only true course. They have been praised and they have been hauled over the coals. Their answer to both has been serious thought about their work and more persistent searching."[24]

The artists singled out for critical attention were Boris Birger, Kirill Mordovin, Vladimir Weisberg, Mikhail Nikonov, and Nikolai Andronov; they are not identified with any particular genre and work with equal interest in still life, portrait painting and murals. Ovsyannikov wrote that some of these young painters, when thinking out big new canvases, "will try out new color combinations, new rhythmic color effects, by painting small abstract sketches"; however "these artists show a common leaning toward the real and the concrete."[25]

The October 1965 issue of *Soviet Life* has an interesting article by another art critic Alexander Baigushev, "New Trends in Art." Not only does he discuss the fact that there are so many more painters to be seen with the rise of new art movements, but he also notices a radical change in the artistic atmosphere. "This is a different viewer who comes to openings of local shows today. He makes bold and independent judgments. He will not take hackneyed art. He expects the artist to assert himself, to have confidence in his own powers."[26]

The Soviet gallery-goer has grown accustomed to look on a visit to any exhibition of contemporary Soviet art as a challenging experience, with much to be seen and evaluated. The Soviet artist, on the other hand, in portraying life in the long-standing tradition of Socialist Realism, has changed perceptibly the form of his work. There is a definite absence of the narrative type of painting reminiscent of the "Peredvizhniki" movement: "The literary handling of subject matter is dying out, and the painter is using the full range of his medium to express himself. This is a result of the long and bitter struggle that the Soviet painter has been waging against the pretentious and the overstated."

There now seem to be new possibilities for artistic expression in the U.S.S.R.; the stereotypes of the personality cult seem to be dying out. However, there is generally "a decided aversion toward slick art, unimaginative detail and photographic portrayal. Every image cries out for the brushwork best suited to it. To do justice to the human character, the artist uses every means at his disposal."[27]

It is a fact that the recent development of Soviet painting has been diverse. Following the international trend, some Soviet painters have turned to abstraction, not always with too much individuality and conviction. However, between the two poles of Socialist Realism and abstraction of today, there is a wide range of vigorous trends which permit us safely to "predict that in the process of stir and change many significant works of art will be born."[28]

Whatever the future of Russian painting may be, it can be said that within its long history of heights and depths, it has proved to have a pronounced elementary accord with life, accomplishing the transition from one to the other with perfect ease and imagination. In its every aspect Russian painting, whether by Rublev or Kandinsky, epitomizes the eternal struggle toward freedom through sublimated creative expression.

NOTES

1. Alexander Benois, *History of Painting in the Nineteenth Century, Russian Painting.* St. Petersburg, 1902, pp. 1-2.
2. *Un Portraitiste Petit-Russien. D.M. Lévitski.* Paris, 1904.
3. Louis Reau, *L'Art Russe de Pierre Grand á nos Jours.* Paris, 1922. Ibid., *L'Art Russe.* Paris, 1945.
4. Rosa Newmarch, *The Russian Arts.* New York, 1916.
5. George Heard Hamilton, *The Art and Architecture of Russia.* London, 1954.
6. Oskar Wulff, *Die Neurussische Kunst.* Augsburg, 1932.
7. Fritz Nemitz, *Die Kunst Russlands. Baukunst, Malerei, Plastik von XI-XIX Jahrh.* Berlin, 1940.
8. Tamara Talbot Rice, *A Concise History of Russian Art.* New York, 1963, p. 200.
9. D. Talbot Rice (Ed.), *Russian Art. Published in Connection with the Exhibition of Russian Art, Belgrave Square.* London, 1935.
10. *Malarstwo Rosyjskie XIV-XX,* May 27-July 15, 1957. Warszawa, Museum Narodowe.
11. *Exhibition of Russian Art, XVIII-XX C.* Peking, 1957.
12. *An Exhibition of Works by Russian and Soviet Artists from the Collections of the Russian Museum in Leningrad,* January 1-March 1, 1959. Royal Academy of Arts, London.
13. *Russian Trade Exhibition.* Coliseum, New York, 1959.
14. *La Peinture Russe et Soviétique,* Mai-Juin, 1960. Musée National d'Art Moderne, Paris.
15. *Exhibition of Soviet Painting and Graphic Arts.* Montreal, Ottawa, Toronto, 1960.
16. *Exhibition of Soviet Graphic Arts,* New York, 1963.
17. John Russell, "London Sees a Half-Length Picture of Russian Art", *Art News,* February, 1959, p. 35.
18. Camilla Gray, *The Great Experiment: Russian Art 1863-1922.* New York, 1962.
19. Alfred H. Barr, Jr., "Russian Icons", *The Arts,* February 1931, p. 358.
20. The most scientific work on this subject is the five-volume edition of *Russian Popular Pictures,* by D. A. Rovinsky, 1900.
21. A. Vatagin, *Selo Palekh.* 1927, #78.
22. Arnold Haskell, *Diaghilev, His Artistic and Private Life.* New York, 1935, p. 87.
23. Herbert Read, "Stravinsky and the Muses," introduction to *Stravinsky and the Dance, A Survey of Ballet Productions 1910-1962.* The Dance Collection of the New York Public Library, New York, 1962, p. 9.
24. *Soviet Life,* April 1965, p. 29.
25. *Ibid.,* p. 29.
26. "New Trends in Art," *Soviet Life,* October 1965, p. 29.
27. *Ibid.,* p. 34.
28. *Ibid.,* p. 34.

IVAN K. AIVAZOVSKY 1817-1900
Seascape. Undated.
Oil on canvas.
Lent by Mr. Samuel J. Kaufman, New York

Sunset. 1876.
Oil on canvas.
Lent by Mr. Igor Sobin,
   Whitestone, New York

ALEKSEY P. ANTROPOV 1716-1895
Portrait of Czar Peter III. ca. 1762.
Oil on canvas.
Lent by Mr. Victor Hammer,
   Hammer Galleries, New York

NICKOLAY I. ARGUNOV 1771-1829
Self Portrait. Undated.
Oil on canvas.
Lent by Mr. Victor Hammer,
   Hammer Galleries, New York

V. ARKHAROV
Holiday. 1966.
Tempera on canvas.
Lent by Mrs. Nina Stevens, New York

MINAS AVETISYAN
Woman of Armenia. Undated.
Oil on canvas.
Private Collection, New York

LEV BAKST 1866-1924
Female Dancer. Undated.
Pencil and watercolor.
Lent by Mr. George Riabov, New York

Fortune Teller. 1900.
Ink and watercolor.
Lent by Mr. and Mrs. A. Herenroth,
   New York

Turk with Scimitar. 1921.
Crayon and watercolor.
Lent by Mr. and Mrs. Boris Pregel, New York

Costume Design for a Priest. Undated.
Gouache.
Lent by Mr. George Riabov, New York

Four Costume Designs for "Tzar Edip".
   Undated.
Gouache.
Lent by Mr. Philip Lynn, New York

Costume Design for a Female Dancer.
   Undated.
Pencil and gouache.
Lent by Mr. Samuel J. Kaufman, New York

Costume Design for a Female Dancer.
   Undated.
Gouache.
Lent by Mr. Samuel J. Kaufman, New York

Costume Design for a Female Dancer.
   Undated.
Crayon and gouache.
Lent by Mrs. Remi Saunder, New York

Costume Design for "Sadko": Boyar. Undated.
Gouache.
Lent by Mr. Ira Spanierman, New York

VASILY BASOV 1918-
Portrait of Chekhov. 1959.
Lithograph.
Lent by Mr. George Riabov, New York

ALEXANDER BENOIS 1870-1960
Illustration for Book. 1910.
Lent by Mr. George Riabov, New York

Costume Design for "Petrouchka":
    Man with Peep Show. Undated.
Watercolor.
Lent by Mr. George Riabov, New York

Costume Design for "Petrouchka":
    A Peasant Woman. Undated.
Watercolor.
Lent by Mr. George Riabov, New York

Costume Design for "Le Pavilion d'Armide":
    A Lady of the Court. 1909.
Watercolor.
Lent by Mr. George Riabov, New York

Costume Design for "Le Pavilion d'Armide":
    A Gentleman of the Court. 1909.
Watercolor.
Lent by Mr. George Riabov, New York

Costume Design for Female Dancer. Undated.
Watercolor.
Lent by Mr. George Riabov, New York

Stage Design for "Pique Dame": Ballroom.
    Undated.
Watercolor.
Lent by Mr. George Riabov, New York

Six Stage Designs for "Giselle". 1910.
Pencil and watercolor.
Lent by Mrs. Alexander Luke, New York

View of the Chapel at Tsarskoye Selo.
    Undated.
Watercolor and ink.
Lent by Mr. and Mrs. Jacques Garvin,
    New York

View of the Waterfront in Novgorod. 1930.
Watercolor and ink.
Lent by Mr. and Mrs. A. Herenroth,
    New York

View of the Bolshoi Theater. 1885.
Watercolor and ink.
Lent by Mr. and Mrs. A. Herenroth,
    New York

View of Uglich. Undated.
Watercolor and ink.
Lent by Mr. George Riabov, New York

View of Murom. Undated.
Watercolor and ink.
Lent by Mr. George Riabov, New York

View of Peterhof. Undated.
Watercolor and ink.
Lent by Mr. George Riabov, New York

*View of St. Petersburg, Monument of
   Nicholas I.* Undated.
Watercolor and ink.
Lent by Mr. George Riabov, New York

View of Pavlovsk. 1923.
Watercolor and ink.
Lent by Mrs. Pauline B. Taylor, New York

View of Pavlovsk, Temple of the Graces.
   1921.
Watercolor and ink.
Lent by Mrs. Pauline B. Taylor, New York

View of the Hermitage Theater. 1922.
Watercolor and ink.
Lent by Mrs. Pauline B. Taylor, New York

View of Oranienbaum. 1923.
Watercolor and crayon.
Lent by Mrs. Pauline B. Taylor, New York

View of Oranienbaum. 1923.
Watercolor and crayon.
Lent by Mrs. Pauline B. Taylor, New York

IVAN BILIBIN 1876-1942
*Illustration for Book: "Tales of a Russian
   Grandmother."* Undated.
Ink.
Lent by Mr. George Riabov, New York

*Cotume Design for "Prince Igor":
   Polovtsian Dancer.* 1930.
Gouache.
Lent by Mr. and Mrs. A. Herenroth,
   New York

Costume Design. 1930.
Gouache.
Lent by Miss Lydia Chaliapin, New York

ALEKSEY P. BOGOLIUBOV 1824-1896
View of a Monastery on the Sea. Undated.
Watercolor.
Lent by Mr. and Mrs. Jacques Garvin,
   New York

VLADIMIR L. BOROVIKOVSKY 1757-1825
Portrait of an Archbishop. Undated.
Oil on canvas.
Lent by Mr. Philip Lynn, New York

Portrait of a Lady. Undated.
Oil on canvas.
Lent by Mr. Peter Tretyakoff, New York

Portrait of an Old Lady. Undated.
Oil on canvas.
Lent by Mr. Philip Lynn, New York

Portrait of a Man. Undated.
Oil on canvas.
Lent by Mr. and Mrs. Jacques Garvin,
   New York

Portrait of a Russian Diplomat. 1805.
Oil on canvas.
Lent by Mr. and Mrs. Boris Pregel, New York

Portrait of Alexander I. Undated.
Oil on canvas.
Lent by Mr. George Riabov, New York

KARL P. BRYULLOV 1799-1852
Portrait of Countess Samoilova. Undated.
Oil on canvas.
Lent by Dr. Armand Hammer, New York

Portrait of Glinka-Mavrin. 1835.
Watercolor.
Lent by Mr. Philip Lynn, New York

Portrait of an Old Lady. 1935.
Watercolor.
Lent by Mr. Philip Lynn, New York

DAVID D. BURLIUK 1882-1967
Farmer and a Horse. Undated.
Oil on canvas.
Lent by Mr. Alexander Liberman, New York

Farmer and a Horse. Undated.
Oil on canvas.
Lent by Mr. Alexander Liberman, New York

MARC CHAGALL 1887-
The Fruit Seller. 1909-10.
Gouache.
Lent by La Boetie, Inc., New York

Rural Scene. 1914.
Gouache.
Lent by La Boetie, Inc., New York

Homage to Gogol. 1917.
Watercolor.
Lent by the Museum of Modern Art,
    New York. Acquired through the
    Lillie P. Bliss Bequest.

FEODOR I. CHALIAPINE 1873-1938
Self Portrait as Boris Godounov. Undated.
Pencil.
Lent by Mr. George Riabov, New York

EVGRAF P. CHEMESOV 1735-1765
*Catherine the Great Mourning the Death of
    Elisabeth.* ca. 1762.
Oil on copper.
Lent by Mr. and Mrs. A. Herenroth,
    New York

NONNA G. CHOTEMOVA 1915-
View of a Church. 1959.
Oil on canvas.
Lent by the Grosvenor Gallery, New York

MSTISLAV V. DOBOUJINSKY 1875-1957
Stage Design for "La Musique Qui Passe."
    1926.
Oil on canvas.
Lent by Mr. Vsevolod Doboujinsky,
    Brooklyn, New York

Costume Design for "Khovantchina": Soldier.
    Undated.
Gouache.
Lent by Mr. George Riabov, New York

Costume Design "Khovantchina": A Noble.
    Undated.
Gouache.
Lent by Mr. George Riabov, New York

Costume Design for "Prince Igor": Chief in Polovtsian Dances. Undated.
Gouache.
Lent by Mr. George Riabov, New York

Costume Design for a Hussar. Undated.
Gouache.
Lent by Mr. George Riabov, New York

Stage Design for "The Marriage". Undated.
Pastel.
Lent by Mrs. Remi Saunder, New York

"The City Visions: Labor". Undated.
Ink and wash.
Lent by Mr. Vsevolod Doboujinsky,
    Brooklyn, New York

"The City Visions: The End". Undated.
Ink and wash.
Lent by Mr. Vsevolod Doboujinsky,
    Brooklyn, New York

View of Chernigov. 1912.
Watercolor and ink.
Lent by Mrs. V. N. Bashkiroff,
    New Preston, Connecticut

View of St. Petersburg. Undated.
Watercolor and ink.
Lent by Mrs. Elena Balieff, New York

ALEXANDRA A. EXTER 1884-1949
Costume Design for Female Dancer. 1925.
Pencil and gouache.
Lent by Mr. George Riabov, New York

Costume Design for Male Dancer. 1925.
Pencil and gouache.
Lent by Mr. George Riabov, New York

Sailing Boat. Undated.
Watercolor.
Lent by the Grosvenor Gallery, London

ROBERT FALK 1886-1958
Forest. Undated.
Oil on paper.
Lent by Mr. and Mrs. Andrei Sedych,
    New York

Sleeping Gypsy. 1920.
Oil on canvas.
Lent by Mrs. Nina Stevens, New York

VLADIMIR FAVORSKY 1886-
*Illustration for A. S. Pushkin's
    "Boris Godounov".* 1949.
Woodcut.
Lent by the Grosvenor Gallery, London

Portrait of Dostoyevsky. 1929.
Woodcut.
Lent by the Grosvenor Gallery, London

Portrait of Mikhail Lermontov. 1931.
Woodcut.
Lent by the Grosvenor Gallery, London

Portrait of Fieldmarshal Kutuzov. Undated.
Woodcut.
Lent by Mr. George Riabov, New York

PAVEL A. FEDOTOV 1815-1852
Portrait of Verigin. Undated.
Watercolor.
Lent by Miss Lydia Chaliapin, New York

A. FONVIZIN 1882-
At a Piano. 1933.
Watercolor.
Lent by Mrs. Nina Stevens, New York

Soirée. 1933.
Watercolor.
Lent by Mrs. Nina Stevens, New York

Luchinskoye. 1935.
Watercolor.
Lent by Mrs. Nina Stevens, New York

Circus Scene. 1955.
Watercolor.
Lent by Mrs. Nina Stevens, New York

Circus Scene. 1955.
Watercolor.
Lent by Mrs. Nina Stevens, New York

Circus Scene. 1955.
Watercolor
Lent by Mrs. Nina Stevens, New York

Nude. 1955.
Watercolor
Lent by Mrs. Nina Stevens, New York

PETER I. GELLER 1962-1953?
*The Local Leader of the Russian Peasantry
    Returns from the Tsar's Coronation.* 1891
Oil on canvas.
Lent by the M. H. de Young Memorial
    Museum, San Francisco

VLADIMIR GHEDIKIAN 1928-
Episode from "The Little Hunchback".
    Undated.
Lent by the Grosvenor Gallery, New York

ALEXANDER Y. GOLOVIN 1863-1930
*Portrait of Feodor Chaliapine as Boris
    Godounov.* Undated.
Gouache.
Lent by Mr. George Riabov, New York

NATHALIE GONTCHAROVA 1881-1962
Self Portrait. 1904.
Oil on canvas.
Lent by Mrs. V. N. Bashkiroff,
    New Preston, Connecticut

Costume Design for "Le Coq d'Or": A Man.
    1914.
Gouache.
Lent by Mr. George Riabov, New York

Danseuses Espagnoles. 1916.
Oil on canvas.
Lent by the Leonard Hutton Galleries,
    New York

Rhapsodie Espagnole. 1916.
Oil on canvas.
Lent by the Leonard Hutton Galleries,
    New York

Archangel. Undated.
Gouache.
Lent by Mr. and Mrs. Boris Pregel, New York

Female Costume Design. Undated.
Pencil and watercolor.
Lent by Mr. and Mrs. Boris Pregel, New York

Stage Design: "The City". Undated.
Gouache.
Lent by Mrs. V. N. Bashkiroff,
    New Preston, Connecticut

Stage Design for "Le Coq d'Or". Undated.
Gouache.
Lent by Mrs. V. N. Bashkiroff,
    New Preston, Connecticut

*Costume Design for "Le Coq d'Or":
    the Magician.* Undated.
Watercolor.
Lent by Mr. George Riabov, New York

*Costume Design for "Le Coq d'Or":
    the Princess.* Undated.
Watercolor.
Lent by Mr. George Riabov, New York

BORIS D. GRIGORIEV 1886-1939
Portrait of the Artist Repin. 1915.
Crayon.
Lent by Mrs. V. N. Bashkiroff,
    New Preston, Connecticut

Russian Village. 1919.
Ink.
Lent by Mr. and Mrs. Roman Tumarkin,
    New York

Russian Village. 1920.
Tempera on canvas.
Lent by Mr. and Mrs. A. Herenroth,
    New York

Portrait of a Woman. 1925.
Oil on canvas.
Lent by Mr. Peter Tretyakoff, New York

Portrait of a Man. Undated.
Oil on canvas.
Lent by Mr. George Riabov, New York

ALEXANDER A. IVANOV 1806-1858
*Study of a Nude Boy for the painting
    "Christ Before the People".* Undated.
Oil on cardboard.
Lent by Mr. and Mrs. Boris Pregel, New York

ALEXEI VON JAWLENSKY 1864-1941
Dunkle Flamme. 1916.
Oil on board mounted on wood.
Lent by the Leonard Hutton Galleries,
    New York

Infanta. 1912-1913.
Oil on wood.
Lent by Mr. and Mrs. Serge Sabarsky, Courtesy
of Leonard Hutton Galleries, New York

Portrait of Marianne von Werefkin. Undated.
Crayon.
Lent by Mr. George Riabov, New York

DAVID KAKABADZE 1889-
Diamonds and Textures. 1920.
Oil on canvas.
Lent by Mrs. Nina Stevens, New York

VASILY V. KANDINSKY 1866-1944
The Snow-covered Isar at Munich. 1902.
Oil on canvas, mounted on wood.
Lent by the Leonard Hutton Galleries,
New York

Murnau, Street and Wagon. 1909.
Oil on wood.
Lent by the Leonard Hutton Galleries,
New York

Theme of the Deluge and the Last Judgment.
1913.
Oil and mixed media on canvas.
Lent by the Leonard Hutton Galleries,
New York

ANATOLI L. KAPLAN 1902-
A Stock Broker. Undated.
Lithograph.
Lent by the Grosvenor Gallery, New York

Anatovka. Undated.
Lithography.
Lent by the Grosvenor Gallery, New York

NICHOLAY A. KASSATKIN 1859-1930
Portrait of a Peasant. 1881.
Oil on canvas.
Lent by Mr. and Mrs. Andrei Sedych,
New York

ALEXANDER KHARITONOV 1931-
Lamenting. 1959.
Oil on canvas.
Lent by Mrs. Nina Stevens, New York

Enchanted House. 1963.
Oil on canvas.
Lent by Mrs. Nina Stevens, New York

Sleeping Kingdom. 1963.
Pencil.
Lent by Mrs. Nina Stevens, New York

N. KHARITONOV
Portrait of Feodor Chaliapine. 1930.
Oil on canvas.
Lent by Mr. Peter Tretyakoff, New York

OREST A. KIPRENSKY 1782-1836
Fishermen. 1910.
Charcoal and chalk.
Lent by Miss Lydia Chaliapin, New York

Ambassador. Undated.
Pencil and ink.
Lent by Mr. George Riabov, New York

Wet Nurse and Child. Undated.
Oil on canvas.
Lent by Mr. Victor Hammer,
    Hammer Galleries, New York

KONSTANTIN A. KOROVIN 1861-1939
Costume Design for "Russlan and Ludmilla":
    Peasant Man. Undated.
Watercolor.
Lent by Mr. George Riabov, New York

Costume Designs for "Le Coq d'Or". Undated.
Watercolor.
    A General.
    A Young Girl.
    Boyar.
    Peasant Woman.
    The Servant to the Tzarina.

    Companion to the Tzarina.
    Merchant.
    Tzar Dodon.
Lent by Mr. George Riabov, New York

Costume Designs for "Khovantchina":
    The People (female). Undated.
        Watercolor.
    The People (male). Undated. Watercolor.
Lent by Mr. George Riabov, New York

Scene in Nice. 1902.
Oil on canvas.
Lent by Mr. Samuel J. Kaufman, New York

Lady at a Terrace Door. 1913.
Oil on canvas.
Lent by Mr. and Mrs. Jacques Garvin,
    New York

Girl Looking out of Window. 1916.
Oil on canvas.
Lent by Mr. and Mrs. Jacques Garvin,
    New York

Paris on a Rainy Night. 1939.
Oil on wood.
Lent by Mr. and Mrs. Jacques Garvin,
    New York.

DIMITRI KRASNOPEVTSEV 1925-
Two Pipes. 1963.
Oil on composition board.
Lent by Mrs. Nina Stevens, New York

The Trunks. 1967.
Oil on canvas.
Lent by Mrs. Nina Stevens, New York

LEO KROPIVNITSKY 1922-
Mask. 1964-1965
Oil on canvas.
Lent by Mrs. Nina Stevens, New York

ARHIP I. KUINDZHI 1842-1910
Sunset. Undated.
Oil and canvas
Lent by Mr. Peter Tretyakoff, New York

ARNOLD B. LAKHOVSKY 1888-1937
View of Pskov. Undated
Oil on canvas.
Lent by Mr. George Riabov, New York

JOHANN-BATISTE LAMPI 1751-1830
Portrait of Empress Catherine the Great.
 Undated.
Oil on canvas.
Lent by A La Vieille Russie, Inc., New York

MIKHAIL F. LARIONIOV 1881-1964
Dunes. 1902.
Oil on canvas.
Lent by Mrs. V. N. Bashkiroff,
 New Preston, Connecticut

Moscow Street Scene. 1902.
Oil on wood.
Lent by Mr. and Mrs. Boris Pregel,
 New York

Bouquet. 1910.
Oil on canvas.
Lent by Mrs. Nina Stevens, New York

Seascape. 1910.
Oil on canvas.
Lent by Mrs. Nina Stevens, New York

Renard the Fox. 1921.
Watercolor.
Lent by Mrs. V. N. Bashkiroff,
 New Preston, Connecticut

Woman's Head. Undated.
Pencil and Oil.
Lent by Mr. Alexander Liberman, New York

Composition. Undated.
Watercolor.
Lent by Mr. and Mrs. Boris Pregel, New York

Woman's Head. Undated.
Pencil and crayon.
Lent by Mr. and Mrs. Jacques Kayaloff,
 New York

NICHOLAY A. LAVROFF 1820-1875
View of the Kremlin. Undated.
Watercolor.
Lent by Mr. George Riabov, New York

View of the Kremlin. Undated.
Watercolor.
Lent by Mr. George Riabov, New York

ISAAK K. LEVITAN 1861-1900
At Night in the Cemetery. 1883.
Chalk.
Lent by Mr. George Riabov, New York

Russian Summer. 1891.
Oil on canvas.
Lent by Mr. and Mrs. Irving Kaufman,
 New York

Big Waters. Undated.
Oil on canvas.
Lent by George Riabov, New York

Landscape. Undated.
Oil on canvas.
Lent by Mr. George Riabov, New York

Still Waters. Undated.
Oil on canvas.
Lent by Mr. George Riabov, New York

DIMITRI G. LEVITSKI 1735-1822
*Portrait of Leonidoff, Ambassador to
    the Court of Egypt.* Undated.
Oil on canvas.
Lent by Mr. and Mrs. André Harley,
    New York

EL LISSITZKY 1890-1947
*Tatlin Building Monument to
    Third International.* 1917.
Collage.
Lent by the Grosvenor Gallery, London

Construction (Proun GK). ca. 1922-23
Gouache.
Lent by the Museum of Modern Art,
    New York

G. LUKOMSKY
View of St. Petersburg. 1906.
Watercolor and pencil.
Lent by Miss Lydia Chaliapin, New York

KONSTANTIN MAKOVSKY 1839-1915
Grandmother's Fairy Tale. Undated.
Oil on canvas.
Lent by Mr. Peter Tretyakoff, New York

VLADIMIR Y. MAKOVSKY 1846-1920
Family Scene. 1888.
Oil on wood.
Lent by Mr. Ira Spanierman, New York

Portrait of a Painter. 1896.
Oil on canvas.
Lent by Mr. George Riabov, New York

KASIMIR MALEVICH 1878-1935
Argentine Polka. 1905.
Gouache.
Lent by Mr. Joachim Jean Aberbach,
    Sands Point, New York

Nymphs. 1908.
Watercolor.
Lent by Mrs. Nina Stevens, New York

Suprematist Construction. 1919-1920.
Watercolor.
Lent by the Grosvenor Gallery, London

FILIP A. MALYAVIN 1869-1939
Girls. Undated.
Oil on canvas.
Lent by Mr. George Riabov, New York

Old Farmer Woman. Undated.
Pencil and crayon.
Lent by Mr. and Mrs. Jacques Garvin,
    New York

Peasant Woman. Undated.
Pencil and crayon.
Lent by Miss Lydia Chaliapin, New York

LYDIA MASTERKOVA 1927-
Composition. 1965.
Oil on canvas.
Lent by Mrs. Nina Steven, New York

Still Life. Undated.
Oil on canvas
Lent by Mrs. Nina Stevens, New York

ERNEST NEIZVESTNY
Drawing in Blue. Undated.
Ink.
Lent by Private Collection, New York

The Angry God. Undated.
Ink.
Lent by Private Collection, New York

GERDA M. NEMENOVA
Head of Gogol. 1959.
Lithograph.
Lent by Mr. George Riabov, New York

VLADIMIR NEMUKHIN 1925-
Islands. 1965.
Watercolor.
Lent by Mrs. Nina Stevens, New York

Solitaire on a Green Table. 1965.
Oil on canvas.
Lent by Mrs. Nina Stevens, New York

Patience (unfinished). 1966.
Oil on canvas.
Lent by Mrs. Nina Stevens, New York

Patience on a Marquetry Table. 1966.
Oil on canvas.
Lent by Mrs. Nina Stevens, New York

MIKHAIL V. NESTEROV 1862-1942
The Painter's Daughter. 1912.
Oil on canvas.
Lent by Mr. and Mrs. Roman Tumarkin,
    New York

In the Cemetery. Undated.
Crayon and watercolor.
Lent by Mr. George Riabov, New York

LEONID O. PASTERNAK 1862-1945
Egg-coloring Scene. 1913.
Pastel.
Lent by Mr. George Riabov, New York

Portrait of a Woman. Undated.
Crayon.
Lent by Mr. Samuel J. Kaufman, New York

ANTOINE PEVSNER 1886-1962
Woman in a Shell with a Bird. 1915-16.
Oil on canvas.
Lent by Mr. and Mrs. Naum Gabo,
    Middlebury, Connecticut

Pears on a Table. 1916.
Oil on canvas.
Lent by Mr. and Mrs. Naum Gabo,
    Middlebury, Connecticut

ALEKSEI PISAREV 1909-

City View, Uglitch. 1960.
Oil on canvas.
Lent by the Grosvenor Gallery, New York

DIMITRI PLAVINSKY 1937-

Voice of Silence. 1960.
Oil on canvas.
Lent by Mrs; Nina Stevens, New York

Hands. 1961.
Ink.
Lent by Mrs. Nina Stevens, New York

Winter Animal. 1964.
Oil and gesso on canvas over wood.
Lent by Mrs. Nina Stevens, New York

Midnight Mass. 1964.
Oil on canvas.
Lent by Mrs. Nina Stevens, New York

Meditation on Ancient Scrolls:
  Muslim Wisdom. 1964.
    Oil, gesso and watercolor on wood.

  Circle Calligraphy. 1964.
    Watercolor and gesso on wood.

  Cruciform Door. 1964.
    Oil and gesso on wood.

  Letter on a Scroll. 1964.
    Oil and gesso on wood.
Lent by Mrs. Nina Stevens, New York

Church Wall. 1965.
Oil on wood bas relief.
Lent by Mrs. Nina Stevens, New York

Figure in Gold. 1965.
Oil on canvas.
Lent by Mrs. Nina Stevens, New York

Man-fish. 1966.
Oil on canvas.
Lent by Mrs. Nina Stevens, New York

Coelacanth. 1966.
Oil on canvas.
Lent by Mrs. Nina Stevens, New York

IVAN P. POKHITONOV 1850-1923

The South of Russia. 1882.
Oil on canvas.
Lent by Mr. George Riabov, New York

VASILI D. POLENOV 1844-1927

The Holy Land. 1879.
Oil on canvas.
Lent by Mr. George Riabov, New York

IVAN POUGNY 1892-1956

Arlequin. Undated.
Oil on canvas.
Lent by Mr. and Mrs. Charles Zadok,
  New York

Arlequin. Undated.
Oil on canvas.
Lent by Mr. and Mrs. Charles Zadok,
  New York

Arlequin. Undated.
Oil on canvas.
Lent by Mr. and Mrs. Jacques Kayaloff,
    New York

Interior of Atelier. Undated.
Oil on canvas.
Lent by Mr. and Mrs. Jacques Kayaloff,
    New York

SERGE PROKOFIEFF 1891-1953
Composition for Constantin. 1933.
Ink.
Lent by Mr. Constantin Alajalov, New York

OSCAR RABIN 1928-
City with Moons. 1962.
Oil on canvas.
Lent by the Grosvenor Gallery, New York

Vinegar and Two Herrings. 1964.
Oil on canvas.
Lent by Mrs. Nina Stevens, New York

Samovar. Undated.
Oil on canvas.
Lent by Mrs. Nina Stevens, New York

ILYA REPIN 1844-1930
Study for "The Volga Boatmen". 1870.
Pencil.
Lent by Mr. and Mrs. A. Herenroth,
    New York

Head. 1876.
Pencil.
Lent by Mr. George Riabov, New York

Portrait of a Girl. 1889.
Oil on canvas.
Lent by Mrs. V. N. Bashkiroff,
    New Preston, Connecticut

*Yuri Ilyitch Repin (the Artist's Son as a
    Young Boy).* 1894.
Oil on canvas.
Lent by Mr. and Mrs. Irving Kaufman,
    New York

Greetings in the Church after the Wedding.
    1894.
Oil on canvas.
Lent by Mr. and Mrs. Irving Kaufman,
    New York

The Year 1905. 1925.
Watercolor.
Lent by Mr. and Mrs. Boris Pregel, New York

Portrait of an Old Man. Undated.
Oil on canvas.
Lent by Mrs. Lydia Kamyshnikoff, New York

Two Figures. Undated.
Oil on canvas.
Lent by Mr. George Riabov, New York

Tolstoy and His Wife. Undated.
Pencil.
Lent by the Grosvenor Gallery, London

Two Cossacks. Undated.
Oil on canvas.
Lent by Mr. Philip Lynn, New York

Study of Heads for "The Cossacks". Undated.
Pencil.
Lent by Mr. and Mrs. Boris Pregel, New York

Cossacks. Undated.
Pencil.
Lent by Mr. George Riabov, New York

ALEXANDER RODCHENKO 1891-1956
Non-Objective Painting. 1919.
Oil on canvas.
Lent by the Museum of Modern Art,
   New York

NICHOLAS ROERICH 1874-1947
Building the Ship. Undated.
Oil on canvas.
Lent by the Nicholas Roerich Museum,
   New York

Wanderer from the Resplendent City.
   Undated.
Oil on canvas.
Lent by the Nicholas Roerich Museum,
   New York

Zwenigorod. Undated.
Oil on canvas.
Lent by the Nicholas Roerich Museum,
   New York

Costume Design for "Ivan the Terrible":
Nobleman. Undated.
Gouache.
Lent by Mr. George Riabov, New York

Costume Designs for "Prince Igor". Undated.
Tempera on canvas.
   Warrior shooting Arrow.
   Maiden with Warrior.
   Warrior with Sword.
   Polovetsky Maiden.
   Polovetsky Camp.
   Maiden with Rose.
Lent by the Nicholas Roerich Museum,
   New York

Stage Designs for "The Rite of Spring".
   Undated.
Tempera on canvas.
   Girl with Garlands
   The Curtain
   Warriors
   Dancers in Bearskins
   The Astrologer
Lent by the Nicholas Roerich Museum,
   New York

Costume Design for "The Rite of Spring":
   A Boyar's Wife. Undated.
Gouache.
Lent by Mr. George Riabov, New York

Costume Design for "The Rite of Spring":
   A Male Dancer. Undated.
Gouache.
Lent by Mr. George Riabov, New York

ALEXANDER C. ROSLIN 1710-1793
Empress Catherine II. 1787.
Engraving after oil by Roslin.
Lent by Mr. George Riabov, New York

ARKADIY A. RYLOV 1870-1939
Winter. 1906.
Oil on canvas.
Lent by Mr. George Riabov, New York

MARTIROS SARYAN 1880-
Kotayk Mountains. 1926.
Oil on canvas.
Lent by Mr. and Mrs. Jacques Kayaloff,
   New York

Ripening Wheat. 1938.
Oil on canvas.
Lent by the Grosvenor Gallery, London

VALENTIN A. SEROV 1865-1911
Portrait of Repin. 1879.
Crayon and pencil.
Lent by Mrs. V. N. Bashkiroff,
   New Preston, Connecticut

Boy, Horse and Haywagon. 1902.
Pencil and watercolor.
Lent by Mrs. V. N. Bashkiroff,
   New Preston, Connecticut

Portrait of K. Korovin and Knyazev. 1907.
Oil on canvas.
Lent by Mr. and Mrs. Boris Chaliapin,
   New York

Portrait of a Boy. Undated.
Oil on canvas.
Lent by Mr. George Riabov, New York

Odessa. Undated.
Oil on canvas.
Lent by Mr. George Riabov, New York

SILVESTER F. SCHEDRIN 1791-1830
Italian Village Road. Undated.
Oil on canvas.
Lent by Mr. Victor Hammer,
   Hammer Galleries, New York

IVAN I. SHISHKIN 1832-1898
Forest Scene. Undated.
Oil on canvas.
Lent by Mr. and Mrs. Stefan Wolynski,
   New York

VASILI SHUKHAEV 1887-
Portrait of Yakovlev. 1921.
Sanquine.
Lent by Mr. Alexander Liberman, New York

Design for "Boris Godounov." 1924.
Gouache.
Lent by Mr. George Riabov, New York

Portrait of Nikita Balieff. 1924.
Sanquine.
Lent by Mrs. Elena Balieff, New York

Village in Normandy. 1929.
Oil on canvas.
Lent by Mr. and Mrs. André Harley,
   New York

Portrait of Sergey Sudeykin. Undated.
Oil on canvas.
Lent by Mr. George Riabov, New York

VASILI SITNIKOV 1915-
Landscape. 1966.
Oil on canvas.
Lent by Mrs. Nina Stevens, New York

PETER I. SOKOLOV
Portrait of Count Edward Hahn. Undated.
Watercolor.
Lent by Mr. Victor Hammer,
   Hammer Galleries, New York

Portrait of Countess Catherine Kutusov.
   Undated.
Watercolor.
Lent by Mr. and Mrs. Kai Winkelhorn,
   New York

KONSTANTIN A. SOMOV 1869-1939
Portrait of Mrs. Hirshman. 1928.
Pastel.
Lent by Mr. and Mrs. André Harley,
   New York

Birches. Undated.
Watercolor.
Lent by Mr. George Riabov, New York

SAVELY A. SORIN 1878-1953
Portrait of Serge Obolensky III. Undated.
Pastel.
Lent by Col. Serge Obolensky, New York

Portrait of Maxim Gorki. Undated.
Oil on canvas.
Lent by the M. H. de Young Memorial
   Museum, San Francisco

SERGEI STEINBERG 1911-
Leningrad. 1959.
Lithograph.
Lent by the ACA Gallery, New York

DIMITRI G. STELLETSKI 1875-1947
Stage Design for "Tsar Theodore Ivanovitch".
   1910.
Oil on canvas.
Lent by Mr. George Riabov, New York

ALEXANDER V. STOUPIN 1776-1861
Young Boy with Leaf. ca. 1820.
Oil on canvas.
Lent by Mr. Victor Hammer,
   Hammer Galleries, New York

SERGEY SUDEYKIN 1882-1946
Portrait of Stravinsky. 1921.
Pencil.
Lent by Mr. George Riabov, New York

Costume Design for a Clown. Undated.
Gouache.
Lent by Mr. Paul Fekula, Elmhurst,
   New York

Costume Design for "New Faces". Undated.
Watercolor.
Lent by Mr. George Riabov, New York

*Fifteen Costume Designs for "The
   Nightingale and the Emperor."* Undated.
Gouache.
Lent by Mrs. Remi Saunder, New York

VASILY I. SURIKOV 1848-1916
Portrait of Repin. 1882.
Watercolor.
Lent by Mr. and Mrs. Andrei Sedych,
    New York

Seascape. Undated.
Oil on canvas.
Lent by Mr. and Mrs. Andrei Sedych,
    New York

Old Woman. Undated.
Oil on cardboard.
Lent by Mrs. V. N. Bashkiroff,
    New Preston, Connecticut

Head of a Young Nun. Undated.
Oil on canvas.
Lent by Mr. and Mrs. Stefan Wolynski,
    New York

JOHANN-GOTTFRIED TANNAUER 1680-1737
Portrait of Peter the Great. 1714.
Engraving.
Lent by Mr. George Riabov, New York

VLADIMIR TATLIN 1885-1953
Head. 1916.
Watercolor.
Lent by the Grosvenor Gallery, London

Standing Woman. 1947.
Oil on wood.
Lent by Mrs. Nina Stevens, New York

Boy Reading. Undated.
Oil on wood.
Lent by the Grosvenor Gallery, London

SERGE TCHEKHONINE 1878-1936
Bandura Player. Undated.
Watercolor.
Lent by Mr. George Riabov, New York

Dancer with Wooden Spoons. Undated.
Watercolor.
Lent by Mr. George Riabov, New York

PAVEL TCHELITCHEW 1898-1957
Male Nude. 1927.
Oil and sand on paper.
Lent by Miss Nan Martin, New York

Seated Multiple Figure. 1927.
Oil and sand on canvas.
Lent by Mr. George Dix, New York

The Actors. 1932.
Ink.
Lent by Mr. George Dix, New York

Love of Polichinella. Undated.
Gouache.
Lent by Mrs. Remi Saunder, New York

*Costume Design for "Orpheus":
    a Male Figure.* Undated.
Gouache.
Lent by Mr. George Riabov, New York

ALEXANDER TISHLER 1898-
Portrait of a Girl. 1936.
Oil on canvas.
Lent by Mrs. Nina Stevens, New York

FEDOR P. TOLSTOI 1783-1873
Equestrian Statue of Peter the Great. 1817.
Silhouette.
Lent by Mr. N. D. Lobanov-Rostovsky,
 New York

VASILI A. TROPININ 1776-1875
Self Portrait. 1843.
Oil on canvas.
Lent by Mr. George Riabov, New York

Self Portrait. Undated.
Oil on canvas.
Lent by Mr. Victor Hammer,
 Hammer Galleries, New York

ALEXEI TYAPUSHKIN 1919-
In the Late Summer, 1960.
Oil on canvas.
Lent by the Grosvenor Gallery, New York

Composition on Black. 1965.
Oil on canvas.
Lent by Mrs. Nina Stevens, New York

OTTO VARAZI ca. 1929-
Bleeding Buffalo, Female. Undated.
Painted cloth mounted on wood.
Lent by Mrs. Nina Stevens, New York

ALEXANDER G. VARNEK 1781-1843
Portrait of the Architect Gromoff. Undated.
Oil on canvas.
Lent by Mr. Victor Hammer,
 Hammer Galleries, New York

VICTOR M. VASNETSOV 1848-1926
Building Moscow. 1900.
Watercolor.
Lent by Mr. and Mrs. A. Herenroth,
 New York

ALEXEI G. VENETSIANOV 1780-1847
Children of Prince Putiatine. Undated.
Oil on canvas.
Lent by Mr. Victor Hammer,
 Hammer Galleries, New York

Girl. Undated.
Oil on canvas.
Lent by Mr. George Riabov, New York

VASILI V. VERESHCHAGIN 1842-1904
Sentry at Shipka. ca. 1880.
Oil on canvas.
Lent by Mr. and Mrs. A. Herenroth,
 New York

The Chapel. Undated.
Oil on canvas.
Lent by Mr. Igor Sobin,
 Whitestone, New York

OREST G. VEREYSKI 1915-
Finland. 1963.
Lithograph.
Lent by Mr. George Riabov, New York

VESHCHILOV
Winter Scene. ca. 1920.
Oil on canvas.
Lent by Mr. George Riabov, New York

E. G. VICKERS
View of Moscow. Undated.
Pencil.
Lent by Mr. George Riabov, New York

SERGEY A. VINOGRADOV 1869-1938
Church Service. Undated.
Oil on cardboard.
Lent by Mr. George Riabov, New York

MAKSIMILIAN A. VOLOSHIN 1877-1931
Crimea. 1930.
Watercolor.
Lent by Mr. George Riabov, New York

VLADIMIR WEISBERG 1924-
Still Life. 1962.
Oil on canvas.
Lent by Mrs. Nina Stevens, New York

Nude. 1963.
Oil on canvas.
Lent by Mrs. Nina Stevens, New York

MARIANNE VON WEREFKIN 1870-1938
Summer Theater. 1910.
Gouache.
Lent by the Leonard Hutton Galleries,
    New York

Portrait of Jawlensky. 1912.
Gouache.
Lent by the Leonard Hutton Galleries,
    New York

ALEXANDER T. YAKOVLEV 1887-1938
Self Portrait. 1929.
Sanquine.
Lent by Mr. Alexander Liberman, New York

Head of a Mongol. 1931.
Sanquine.
Lent by Mr. George Riabov, New York

Kabuki. Undated.
Sanquine.
Lent by Mrs. William Wasserman,
    New York

KONSTANTIN F. YUON 1875-1958?
Country Holiday. Undated.
Lent by Mr. and Mrs. Jacques Garvin,
    New York

View of Troitzky Monastery. Undated.
Gouache.
Lent by Mr. and Mrs. Jacques Garvin,
New York

ANATOLI ZVEREV 1931-
Summer. 1965.
Oil on paper.
Lent by Mrs. Nina Stevens, New York

PORTRAIT MINIATURES

ANONYMOUS
Anne I. ca. 1735.
Enamel.
Lent by Mr. and Mrs. A. Herenroth,
    New York

ANONYMOUS
Catherine I. ca. 1725.
Enamel.
Lent by Mr. and Mrs. A. Herenroth,
    New York

ANONYMOUS
Peter the Great. ca. 1707.
Enamel.
Lent by Mr. and Mrs. A. Herenroth,
    New York

ANONYMOUS
Empress Elizabeth. 18th century.
Ivory.
Lent by A La Vieille Russie, Inc., New York

ANONYMOUS
Tsar Paul I. 18th century.
Enamel.
Lent by A La Vieille Russie, Inc., New York

ANONYMOUS
Portrait of M. Kutuzov. 18th century.
Ivory.
Lent by Mr. and Mrs. Kai Winkelhorn,
    New York

C. BECHON
Fieldmarshal Suvorov. 1795.
Ivory.
Lent by Mr. and Mrs. Kai Winkelhorn,
    New York

IZIEDINOFF
Empress Alexandra. 19th century.
Ivory.
Lent by Mr. and Mrs. A. Herenroth,
    New York

Nicholas II. 19th century.
Ivory.
Lent by Mr. and Mrs. A. Herenroth,
    New York

RAULOV
Wife of the Artist Aivazovsky. ca. 1860.
Ivory.
Lent by Mr. and Mrs. A. Herenroth,
    New York

RITT
Prince Dolgorukov. ca. 1797.
Ivory.
Lent by Mr. and Mrs. A. Herenroth,
    New York

ALOIS G. ROCKSTUHL. 1798-1887
Tsar Alexander II. 1864.
Enamel.
Lent by A La Vieille Russie, Inc., New York

P. ROSSI
Tsar Alexander I. 1804.
Ivory.
Lent by Mr. and Mrs. A. Herenroth,
New York

I. WINBERG
Tsar Nicholas I. ca. 1850.
Ivory.
Lent by Mr. and Mrs. A. Herenroth,
New York

Empress Alexandra. ca. 1850.
Ivory.
Lent by Mr. and Mrs. A. Herenroth,
New York

Member of the Royal Family. ca. 1850.
Ivory.
Lent by Mr. and Mrs. A. Herenroth,
New York

Member of the Royal Family. ca. 1850.
Ivory.
Lent by Mr. and Mrs. A. Herenroth,
New York

MISCELLANY
Lacquered wood box from Palekh. 1927
Lent by Mr. George Riabov, New York

*Enameled bowl with miniature portrait of
Count Apraxine.* ca. 1710.
Lent by Mr. and Mrs. A. Herenroth,
New York

Lubok. (folk print).
Lent by Mr. Alexander Liberman, New York

*Hand-painted book illustrations of the
Wedding of Tsar Mikhail Feodorovich.*
1810.
Lent by Mr. and Mrs. A. Herenroth,
New York

Hand-colored Bible Pages. 17th century.
Woodcuts.
Lent by Mr. George Riabov, New York

ANDREI GREKOV
Armorial of Good Duke Paul. 1769.
Hand-painted Vellum.
Lent by Mr. and Mrs. A. Herenroth,
New York

VASILY KOREN
Bible Page. 1696. Hand-colored woodcut.
Lent by Mr. George Riabov, New York

OLEARIOUS
Map of Moscow's Kremlin. 18th century.
Etching.
Lent by Mr. George Riabov, New York

D. A. ROVINSKY. 1824-1895
Book of Folk Prints. Published in 1900.
Lent by Mr. and Mrs. A. Herenroth,
New York

ANDREI N. VORONIKHIN. 1759-1814
Book containing ten original drawings.
Undated.
Lent by Mr. George Riabov, New York

ICONS

14TH CENTURY

Our Lady's Protection. Bronze.
Lent by Mr. George Riabov, New York

15TH CENTURY

Iconostasis. Tempera on wood.
Lent by Miss Irina Nelidow, St. Louis, and
   Mrs. Guido Pantaleoni, Bronxville,
   New York

The Conception of John the Baptist.
   Tempera on wood.
Lent by A. La Vieille Russie, Inc., New York

St. Nicholas Novgorod. Tempera on wood.
Lent by Mr. George Riabov, New York

Christ Pantocrator. Tempera on wood.
Lent by Mrs. Nina Stevens, New York

The Archangel Michael. Tempera on wood.
Lent by Mrs. Nina Stevens, New York

The Archangel Gabriel. Tempera on wood.
Lent by Mrs. Nina Stevens, New York

16TH CENTURY

An Angel. Tempera on wood.
Lent by the Brooklyn Museum, New York

St. John the Evangelist. Tempera on wood.
Lent by the Brooklyn Museum, New York

The Virgin. Tempera on wood.
Lent by the Brooklyn Museum, New York

The Month of September. Tempera on wood.
Lent by Miss Claudia Lyon, New York

Three Rows of Saints. Tempera on wood.
Lent by Miss Claudia Lyon, New York

The Annunciation. Tempera on wood.
Lent by Mr. Paul Fekula, Elmhurst,
   New York

The Nativity. Tempera on wood.
Lent by Mr. Paul Fekula, Elmhurst,
   New York

The Baptism. Tempera on wood.
Lent by Mr. Paul Fekula, Elmhurst,
   New York

The Entry into Jerusalem. Tempera on wood.
Lent by Mr. Paul Fekula, Elmhurst,
   New York

The Resurrection. Tempera on wood.
Lent by Mr. Paul Fekula, Elmhurst,
   New York

Christ the Saviour. 1592. Bronze.
Lent by Mr. George Riabov, New York

Christ. Tempera on wood.
Lent by Mr. George Riabov, New York

*The Presentation of the Holy Virgin
   in the Temple.* Tempera on wood.
Lent by Mr. George Riabov, New York

The Transfiguration. Tempera on wood.
Lent by Mr. George Riabov, New York

St. George. Tempera on wood.
Lent by Mrs. Nina Stevens, New York

Our Lady of Evsimansk. Tempera on wood.
Lent by A La Vieille Russie, Inc., New York

Our Lady of the Sign. Tempera on wood.
Lent by A La Vieille Russie, Inc., New York

St. Nicholas the Warrior of Mojhaisk. Bronze.
Lent by A La Vieille Russie, Inc., New York

Pair of Royal Sanctuary Doors. Tempera
on wood.
Lent by A La Vieille Russie, Inc., New York

17TH CENTURY
Iconostasis. Painted by Procopiy Chirin.
Tempera on wood.
Lent by Mr. Paul Fekula, Elmhurst,
New York

The Resurrection. Tempera on wood.
Lent by Mr. Paul Fekula, Elmhurst,
New York

The Descent into Hell; The Resurrection.
Tempera on wood.
Lent by Mr. George Riabov, New York

St. Nicholas. Copper.
Lent by Mrs. Nina Stevens, New York

The Nativity. Copper.
Lent by Mrs. Nina Stevens, New York

St. George. Enamel on bronze.
Lent by A La Vieille Russie, Inc., New York

*Scenes from the Life of St. Catherine
the Great Martyr.* Tempera on wood.
Lent by A La Vieille Russie, Inc., New York

Calendar of the Festival Days of Great Lent.
Tempera on wood.
Lent by A La Vieille Russie, Inc., New York

The Ascension of Christ. Tempera on wood.
Lent by A La Vieille Russie, Inc., New York

Panagia: *Persecution of Christ.* Enamel and
gilt metal.
Lent by A La Vieille Russie, Inc., New York

18TH CENTURY
The Last Judgement. Tempera on wood.
Lent by Mr. Paul Fekula, Elmhurst,
New York

St. George. Enamel on copper.
Lent by Mrs. Nina Stevens, New York

The Crucifixion. Enamel on bronze.
Lent by Mrs. Nina Stevens, New York

An Archangel. Enamel on bronze.
Lent by Mrs. Nina Stevens, New York

The Annunciation. Brass.
Lent by Mrs. Nina Stevens, New York

St. George. Brass.
Lent by Mrs. Nina Stevens, New York

The Dëesis; The Trinity; Saints. Brass.
Lent by Mrs. Nina Stevens, New York

The Crucifixion. Enamel on bronze.
Lent by A La Vieille Russie, Inc., New York

19TH CENTURY
Christ, Our Lady and John the Baptist.
    Tempera on wood.
Lent by Mrs. Nina Stevens, New York

SELECTED BIBLIOGRAPHY

Benois, A., *The Russian School of Painting.* St. Petersburg, 1904 (In Russian)

Yaremich, S., *M. A. Vrubel.* Moscow, 1911 (In Russian)

Grabar, I., *Serov, his Life and Work.* Moscow, 1913 (In Russian)

Newmarch, R., *The Russian Arts.* London, 1916

Muratov, P., *L'Ancienne Peinture Russe.* Rome and Prague, 1925

Wulff, O. and Alpatov. M., *Denkmaler der Iconenmalerei.* Hellerau bei Dresden, 1925

Kondakov, N., *The Russian Icon.* 4 vols. Prague, 1928-33 (In Russian)

Bakushinsky, A., *The Art of Palekh.* Moscow-Leningrad, 1934 (In Russian)

Polovtsoff, A., *Russian Exhibition Gossip.* London, 1935

Rice, D. T., *Russian Art.* London, 1935

Lebedev, G., *Russian Painting in the early 18th century.* Moscow, 1938 (In Russian)

Chen, J., *Soviet Art and Artists.* London, 1944

Lukomsky, G. K., *History of Modern Russian Painting.* London, 1945

Rice, D. Talbot, *Russian Icons.* London and New York, 1947

Grabar, I., *Repin.* 2 vols. Moscow-Leningrad, 1948-49 (In Russian)

Hamilton, G. H., *The Art and Architecture of Russia.* London, 1954

Shcherbatov, Serge, *An Artist in Vanished Russia.* New York, 1955 (In Russian)

U.N.E.S.C.O. World Art Series, *Early Russian Icons.* New York, 1958

Gray, C., *The Great Experiment: Russian Art 1863-1922.* New York, 1962

Gerhard, H. P., *Welt der Ikonen.* Recklinghausen, 1963

Rice, T. Talbot, *A Concise History of Russian Art.* London, 1964

Grabar, I., *History of Russian Art.* 15 vols. Moscow, 1950's-1960's (In Russian)